SEE 🙂 THE GOOD

Journal

SEE THE GOOD

Journal

ZACH WINDAHL

BETHANYHOUSE
a division of Baker Publishing Group
Minneapolis, Minnesota

Published by Bethany House Publishers
Minneapolis, Minnesota
www.bethanyhouse.com

Bethany House Publishers is a division of
Baker Publishing Group, Grand Rapids, Michigan

Printed in China

ISBN 978-0-7642-4166-6 (cloth)
ISBN 978-1-4934-4245-4 (ebook)

Cover design by Dan Pitts

Baker Publishing Group publications use paper produced from sustainable forestry practices and post-consumer waste whenever possible.

23 24 25 26 27 28 29   7 6 5 4 3 2 1

WELCOME to the
See the Good Journal!

Have you been feeling worn-out lately?

Tired?

Overwhelmed?

You look at the news and it seems like the world is falling apart?

Like "bad days" are much more common than good ones lately, making it hard to be grateful?

I get it. Life is pretty wild right now, but I believe God is still moving all around us. I believe there is so much wonder and awe all around if you know where to look for it.

Over the next ninety days, our goal is to help you become more grateful, and in return, fill you with joy, hope, and faith for all that God is doing in your life.

My name is Zach Windahl, and I believe that it is our role as believers to find God in everything—to find the good all around us and call it out. And share it with others. We are supposed to be spreading heaven on earth. Impacting the world in a positive way. When you grow in your faith, this is who you should be becoming.

In ancient Judaism there was a major emphasis on gratitude. They would actually make it a point to thank God one hundred times every single day from the moment they woke up until the moment they went to bed.

God, thank you for my eyes to see.

Thank you for my organs working properly.

Thank you for another breath in my lungs.

For the sunshine.

For the hands that made this meal.

They were short prayers to always keep God at the forefront of their minds, because they knew all good things came from him.

And I think we have a lot to learn from this practice. How different would life be for us if we saw all the good things God is doing instead of focusing on our circumstances?

No matter what may happen to us, good or bad, we can focus on the one who gives us strength to enjoy another day. It's a big-picture perspective. We know that God will work everything out for our good eventually.

The apostle Paul taught the Philippian church to "fix your thoughts on what is true, and honorable, and right, and pure, and lovely, and admirable. Think about things that are excellent and worthy of praise" (4:8).

I don't know about you, but I can surely think of some things that are lovely and excellent and worthy of praise. If we fill our minds with the things of God, we don't have room for negative thoughts. We aren't entitled to anything. Everything is a gift.

Water is a gift.

My eyes are a gift.

Being saved is a gift.

Every breath with a "thank you" attached to it is a gift.

There are countless things we can be grateful for if we only learn to open our eyes. We don't need to recite one hundred things that we are grateful for each day, but we can start with three.

The *See the Good Journal* was created to help you see the good in every day and grow closer to God in the process. I know you're going to be blessed by it.

Love you all.

—Zach Windahl

Growing Together

WE UNDERSTAND that being consistent with something for ninety days is really hard. In reality, most people won't fill this out every single day. And that's okay. Take it one day at a time. If you miss one day or twelve, pick back up where you left off. Consistency is going to be key here.

Also, we highly recommend doing this with a friend—an accountability partner, if you will. Choosing to improve your personal well-being is much easier when you have someone else doing it alongside you.

Who is one person you would like to have join you on this journey?

We made a worship playlist for you to enjoy
while journaling every day.

Available on Apple Music and Spotify.

How This Works

THE *SEE THE GOOD JOURNAL* serves as a personal check-in every morning and evening; it sets you up for success as you go about your day.

MORNING CHECK-IN

We believe in a holistic approach to life, so the *See the Good Journal* begins with a spiritual, mental, and physical check-in. Being aware of how you are feeling helps acknowledge areas in your life that may need some additional attention.

GRATITUDE

We believe having an attitude of gratitude is one of the most important ways to boost your joy. So every day we suggest thanking God for a minimum of three things in your life.

BLESS OTHERS

You and I are blessed to be a blessing. We believe taking actionable steps to show others the love of Jesus is one of the best ways to live a kingdom lifestyle. This could be anywhere from sending a text to someone you appreciate, buying a stranger a cup of coffee, or genuinely asking someone how their day is going.

TODAY I GET TO

We believe shifting our mindset from "Today I *have* to" to "Today I *get* to" makes our daily tasks much more manageable and enjoyable. But really, this is meant to just serve as your to-do list for the day.

PRAYER REQUESTS

We believe writing out our prayer requests is beneficial for staying focused during prayer. Each day, write at least one thing that you have been praying for lately.

JOURNAL

We have included a short journal prompt every day to help increase your hope and start the day on a good note.

EVENING CHECK-IN

Every day ends with another holistic check-in to hold yourself accountable as you grow closer to God.

SEEING THE GOOD

We understand that some days are a little harder than others, but we recommend always trying to find God in the midst of the madness. So this question is meant to bring you in line with what God is doing in your life.

BETTER TOMORROW

It is our goal to be a little bit better every single day. We believe having a plan for the next day before you go to bed is a great way to wake up in a positive, peaceful mindset.

CURRENTLY . . .

Where am I in my walk with God?

1   2   3   4   5

_____

_____

_____

Do I see God moving in my life? How so?

1   2   3   4   5

_____

_____

_____

Am I hopeful of the future? What are my plans?

1   2   3   4   5

_____

_____

_____

Do I positively influence my community? How so?

1   2   3   4   5

_____

_____

_____

_____

How is my mental health?

1   2   3   4   5

_____

_____

_____

How do I feel physically?

1   2   3   4   5

_____

_____

_____

What are my ninety-day goals?

_____

_____

_____

_____

How will I get there?

_____

_____

_____

_____

_____

_____

MORNING

DATE: _____

How do I feel?

Spiritually	1	2	3	4	5
Mentally	1	2	3	4	5
Physically	1	2	3	4	5

I'm grateful for . . .

1. _____

2. _____

3. _____

What am I most excited about today?

_____

_____

Who can I bless/encourage today?

_____

_____

Today I get to . . .

Morning

_____

Afternoon

_____

Evening

_____

Prayer requests

_____

_____

_____

Here's how I have witnessed God move in my life recently . . .

_____

_____

_____

_____

NIGHT

I felt closer to God today.   ☐ Yes ☐ No

I had a positive thought life today.   ☐ Yes ☐ No

I ate healthy and/or worked out today.   ☐ Yes ☐ No

Where did I see God moving in my life today?

_____

_____

_____

How can I be better tomorrow?

_____

_____

_____

MORNING

How do I feel?

Spiritually	1	2	3	4	5
Mentally	1	2	3	4	5
Physically	1	2	3	4	5

I'm grateful for . . .

1. _____

2. _____

3. _____

What am I most excited about today?

_____

_____

Who can I bless/encourage today?

_____

_____

Today I get to . . .

Morning

_____

Afternoon

_____

Evening

_____

Prayer requests

_____

_____

_____

Here is one negative experience that turned into something good.

_____

_____

_____

_____

NIGHT

I felt closer to God today.   ☐ Yes   ☐ No

I had a positive thought life today.   ☐ Yes   ☐ No

I ate healthy and/or worked out today.   ☐ Yes   ☐ No

Where did I see God moving in my life today?

_____

_____

_____

How can I be better tomorrow?

_____

_____

_____

MORNING

How do I feel?

Spiritually	1	2	3	4	5
Mentally	1	2	3	4	5
Physically	1	2	3	4	5

I'm grateful for . . .

1. _____

2. _____

3. _____

What am I most excited about today?

_____

_____

Who can I bless/encourage today?

_____

_____

Today I get to . . .

Morning

_____

Afternoon

_____

Evening

_____

Prayer requests

_____

_____

_____

This person has impacted my life without their knowing it, and here's how . . .

_____

_____

_____

_____

NIGHT

I felt closer to God today. ☐ Yes ☐ No

I had a positive thought life today. ☐ Yes ☐ No

I ate healthy and/or worked out today. ☐ Yes ☐ No

Where did I see God moving in my life today?

_____

_____

_____

How can I be better tomorrow?

_____

_____

_____

MORNING

DATE: _____

How do I feel?

Spiritually	1	2	3	4	5
Mentally	1	2	3	4	5
Physically	1	2	3	4	5

I'm grateful for . . .

1. _____

2. _____

3. _____

What am I most excited about today?

_____

_____

Who can I bless/encourage today?

_____

_____

Today I get to . . .

Morning

_____

Afternoon

_____

Evening

_____

Prayer requests

_____

_____

_____

These people have impacted my life the most this year:

_____

_____

_____

_____

NIGHT

I felt closer to God today.	☐ Yes	☐ No
I had a positive thought life today.	☐ Yes	☐ No
I ate healthy and/or worked out today.	☐ Yes	☐ No

Where did I see God moving in my life today?

_____

_____

_____

How can I be better tomorrow?

_____

_____

_____

MORNING

How do I feel?

Spiritually	1	2	3	4	5
Mentally	1	2	3	4	5
Physically	1	2	3	4	5

I'm grateful for . . .

1. _____

2. _____

3. _____

What am I most excited about today?

_____

_____

Who can I bless/encourage today?

_____

_____

Today I get to . . .

Morning

_____

Afternoon

_____

Evening

_____

Prayer requests

_____

_____

_____

This is what I believe it means to be there for someone . . .

_____

_____

_____

_____

NIGHT

I felt closer to God today. ☐ Yes ☐ No

I had a positive thought life today. ☐ Yes ☐ No

I ate healthy and/or worked out today. ☐ Yes ☐ No

Where did I see God moving in my life today?

_____

_____

_____

How can I be better tomorrow?

_____

_____

_____

MORNING

How do I feel?

Spiritually	1	2	3	4	5
Mentally	1	2	3	4	5
Physically	1	2	3	4	5

I'm grateful for . . .

1. _____

2. _____

3. _____

What am I most excited about today?

_____

_____

Who can I bless/encourage today?

_____

_____

Today I get to . . .

Morning

_____

Afternoon

_____

Evening

_____

Prayer requests

_____

_____

_____

I'm grateful for these three people:

_____

_____

_____

_____

NIGHT

I felt closer to God today.   ☐ Yes ☐ No

I had a positive thought life today.   ☐ Yes ☐ No

I ate healthy and/or worked out today.   ☐ Yes ☐ No

Where did I see God moving in my life today?

_____

_____

_____

How can I be better tomorrow?

_____

_____

_____

MORNING

How do I feel?

Spiritually	1	2	3	4	5
Mentally	1	2	3	4	5
Physically	1	2	3	4	5

I'm grateful for . . .

1. _____

2. _____

3. _____

What am I most excited about today?

_____

_____

Who can I bless/encourage today?

_____

_____

Today I get to . . .

Morning

_____

Afternoon

_____

Evening

_____

Prayer requests

_____

_____

_____

This is the accomplishment I'm most proud of:

_____

_____

_____

_____

NIGHT

I felt closer to God today.   ☐ Yes ☐ No

I had a positive thought life today.   ☐ Yes ☐ No

I ate healthy and/or worked out today.   ☐ Yes ☐ No

Where did I see God moving in my life today?

_____

_____

_____

How can I be better tomorrow?

_____

_____

_____

WEEKLY REFLECTION

In what ways did I see God move this week?

_____

_____

What is God teaching me right now?

_____

_____

Did I spend my time wisely this week?

_____

_____

Did I enjoy my life this week?

_____

_____

How can I be a blessing to someone next week?

_____

_____

How can I improve my relationship with God next week?

_____

_____

PRAISE REPORTS

_____

_____

God is good.
And all
of life
is a gift.

MORNING

How do I feel?

Spiritually	1	2	3	4	5
Mentally	1	2	3	4	5
Physically	1	2	3	4	5

I'm grateful for . . .

1. _____

2. _____

3. _____

What am I most excited about today?

_____

_____

Who can I bless/encourage today?

_____

_____

Today I get to . . .

Morning

_____

Afternoon

_____

Evening

_____

Prayer requests

_____

_____

_____

Define joy.

_____

_____

_____

_____

NIGHT

I felt closer to God today.   ☐ Yes   ☐ No

I had a positive thought life today.   ☐ Yes   ☐ No

I ate healthy and/or worked out today.   ☐ Yes   ☐ No

Where did I see God moving in my life today?

_____

_____

_____

How can I be better tomorrow?

_____

_____

_____

MORNING

How do I feel?

Spiritually	1	2	3	4	5
Mentally	1	2	3	4	5
Physically	1	2	3	4	5

I'm grateful for . . .

1. _____

2. _____

3. _____

What am I most excited about today?

_____

_____

Who can I bless/encourage today?

_____

_____

Today I get to . . .

Morning

_____

Afternoon

_____

Evening

_____

Prayer requests

_____

_____

_____

If I'm having a bad day, this is the way in which I'd want my loved ones to help me:

_____

_____

_____

_____

NIGHT

I felt closer to God today.   ☐ Yes   ☐ No

I had a positive thought life today.   ☐ Yes   ☐ No

I ate healthy and/or worked out today.   ☐ Yes   ☐ No

Where did I see God moving in my life today?

_____

_____

_____

How can I be better tomorrow?

_____

_____

_____

MORNING

How do I feel?

Spiritually	1	2	3	4	5
Mentally	1	2	3	4	5
Physically	1	2	3	4	5

I'm grateful for . . .

1. _____

2. _____

3. _____

What am I most excited about today?

_____

_____

Who can I bless/encourage today?

_____

_____

Today I get to . . .

Morning

_____

Afternoon

_____

Evening

_____

Prayer requests

_____

_____

_____

What makes you feel at home?

_____

_____

_____

_____

NIGHT

I felt closer to God today.   ☐ Yes   ☐ No

I had a positive thought life today.   ☐ Yes   ☐ No

I ate healthy and/or worked out today.   ☐ Yes   ☐ No

Where did I see God moving in my life today?

_____

_____

_____

How can I be better tomorrow?

_____

_____

_____

MORNING

How do I feel?

Spiritually	1	2	3	4	5
Mentally	1	2	3	4	5
Physically	1	2	3	4	5

I'm grateful for . . .

1. _____

2. _____

3. _____

What am I most excited about today?

_____

_____

Who can I bless/encourage today?

_____

_____

Today I get to . . .

Morning

_____

Afternoon

_____

Evening

_____

Prayer requests

This is one nice thing that I've done for someone that really stuck with me . . .

NIGHT

I felt closer to God today.	☐ Yes ☐ No
I had a positive thought life today.	☐ Yes ☐ No
I ate healthy and/or worked out today.	☐ Yes ☐ No

Where did I see God moving in my life today?

How can I be better tomorrow?

MORNING

How do I feel?

Spiritually	1	2	3	4	5
Mentally	1	2	3	4	5
Physically	1	2	3	4	5

I'm grateful for . . .

1. _____

2. _____

3. _____

What am I most excited about today?

_____

_____

Who can I bless/encourage today?

_____

_____

Today I get to . . .

Morning

_____

Afternoon

_____

Evening

_____

Prayer requests

_____

_____

_____

This is a little insight into my favorite holiday . . .

_____

_____

_____

_____

NIGHT

I felt closer to God today.   ☐ Yes   ☐ No

I had a positive thought life today.   ☐ Yes   ☐ No

I ate healthy and/or worked out today.   ☐ Yes   ☐ No

Where did I see God moving in my life today?

_____

_____

_____

How can I be better tomorrow?

_____

_____

_____

MORNING

How do I feel?

Spiritually	1	2	3	4	5
Mentally	1	2	3	4	5
Physically	1	2	3	4	5

I'm grateful for . . .

1. _____

2. _____

3. _____

What am I most excited about today?

_____

_____

Who can I bless/encourage today?

_____

_____

Today I get to . . .

Morning

_____

Afternoon

_____

Evening

_____

Prayer requests

_____

_____

_____

What is more important: progress or perfection?

_____

_____

_____

_____

NIGHT

I felt closer to God today.   ☐ Yes   ☐ No

I had a positive thought life today.   ☐ Yes   ☐ No

I ate healthy and/or worked out today. ☐ Yes   ☐ No

Where did I see God moving in my life today?

_____

_____

_____

How can I be better tomorrow?

_____

_____

_____

MORNING

How do I feel?

Spiritually	1	2	3	4	5
Mentally	1	2	3	4	5
Physically	1	2	3	4	5

I'm grateful for . . .

1. _____

2. _____

3. _____

What am I most excited about today?

_____

_____

Who can I bless/encourage today?

_____

_____

Today I get to . . .

Morning

_____

Afternoon

_____

Evening

_____

Prayer requests

_____

_____

_____

This is one cause I am passionate about:

_____

_____

_____

NIGHT

I felt closer to God today.   ☐ Yes   ☐ No

I had a positive thought life today.   ☐ Yes   ☐ No

I ate healthy and/or worked out today.   ☐ Yes   ☐ No

Where did I see God moving in my life today?

_____

_____

How can I be better tomorrow?

_____

_____

WEEKLY REFLECTION

In what ways did I see God move this week?

What is God teaching me right now?

Did I spend my time wisely this week?

Did I enjoy my life this week?

How can I be a blessing to someone next week?

How can I improve my relationship with God next week?

PRAISE REPORTS

See the good.

See the good.

See the good.

MORNING

How do I feel?

Spiritually	1	2	3	4	5
Mentally	1	2	3	4	5
Physically	1	2	3	4	5

I'm grateful for . . .

1.

2.

3.

What am I most excited about today?

Who can I bless/encourage today?

Today I get to . . .

Morning

Afternoon

Evening

Prayer requests

_____

_____

_____

Here's something I'm looking forward to:

_____

_____

_____

_____

NIGHT

I felt closer to God today. ☐ Yes ☐ No

I had a positive thought life today. ☐ Yes ☐ No

I ate healthy and/or worked out today. ☐ Yes ☐ No

Where did I see God moving in my life today?

_____

_____

_____

How can I be better tomorrow?

_____

_____

_____

MORNING

How do I feel?

Spiritually	1	2	3	4	5
Mentally	1	2	3	4	5
Physically	1	2	3	4	5

I'm grateful for . . .

1. _____

2. _____

3. _____

What am I most excited about today?

_____

_____

Who can I bless/encourage today?

_____

_____

Today I get to . . .

Morning

_____

Afternoon

_____

Evening

_____

Prayer requests

_____

_____

_____

The best lesson I've learned from being in a relationship is . . .

_____

_____

_____

_____

NIGHT

I felt closer to God today.   ☐ Yes   ☐ No

I had a positive thought life today.   ☐ Yes   ☐ No

I ate healthy and/or worked out today. ☐ Yes   ☐ No

Where did I see God moving in my life today?

_____

_____

_____

How can I be better tomorrow?

_____

_____

_____

MORNING

How do I feel?

Spiritually	1	2	3	4	5
Mentally	1	2	3	4	5
Physically	1	2	3	4	5

I'm grateful for . . .

1. _____

2. _____

3. _____

What am I most excited about today?

_____

_____

Who can I bless/encourage today?

_____

_____

Today I get to . . .

Morning

_____

Afternoon

_____

Evening

_____

Prayer requests

_____

_____

_____

When I reflect back, I think the best thing about the way I was raised
is . . .

_____

_____

_____

_____

NIGHT

I felt closer to God today.   ☐ Yes ☐ No

I had a positive thought life today.   ☐ Yes ☐ No

I ate healthy and/or worked out today.   ☐ Yes ☐ No

Where did I see God moving in my life today?

_____

_____

_____

How can I be better tomorrow?

_____

_____

_____

MORNING

How do I feel?

Spiritually	1	2	3	4	5
Mentally	1	2	3	4	5
Physically	1	2	3	4	5

I'm grateful for . . .

1. _____

2. _____

3. _____

What am I most excited about today?

_____

_____

Who can I bless/encourage today?

_____

_____

Today I get to . . .

Morning

_____

Afternoon

_____

Evening

_____

Prayer requests

_____

_____

_____

This is my greatest life lesson.

_____

_____

_____

_____

NIGHT

I felt closer to God today. ☐ Yes ☐ No

I had a positive thought life today. ☐ Yes ☐ No

I ate healthy and/or worked out today. ☐ Yes ☐ No

Where did I see God moving in my life today?

_____

_____

_____

How can I be better tomorrow?

_____

_____

_____

MORNING

How do I feel?

Spiritually	1	2	3	4	5
Mentally	1	2	3	4	5
Physically	1	2	3	4	5

I'm grateful for . . .

1. _____

2. _____

3. _____

What am I most excited about today?

_____

_____

Who can I bless/encourage today?

_____

_____

Today I get to . . .

Morning

_____

Afternoon

_____

Evening

_____

Prayer requests

_____

_____

_____

My biggest source of happiness is . . .

_____

_____

_____

_____

NIGHT

I felt closer to God today.   ☐ Yes   ☐ No

I had a positive thought life today.   ☐ Yes   ☐ No

I ate healthy and/or worked out today.   ☐ Yes   ☐ No

Where did I see God moving in my life today?

_____

_____

_____

How can I be better tomorrow?

_____

_____

_____

MORNING

How do I feel?

Spiritually	1	2	3	4	5
Mentally	1	2	3	4	5
Physically	1	2	3	4	5

I'm grateful for . . .

1. _____

2. _____

3. _____

What am I most excited about today?

_____

_____

Who can I bless/encourage today?

_____

_____

Today I get to . . .

Morning

_____

Afternoon

_____

Evening

_____

Prayer requests

_____
_____
_____

This is how I got through the last "bad day" I had:

_____
_____
_____
_____

NIGHT

I felt closer to God today.　　　　　　☐ Yes　☐ No

I had a positive thought life today.　　☐ Yes　☐ No

I ate healthy and/or worked out today.　☐ Yes　☐ No

Where did I see God moving in my life today?

_____
_____
_____

How can I be better tomorrow?

_____
_____
_____

MORNING

How do I feel?

Spiritually	1	2	3	4	5
Mentally	1	2	3	4	5
Physically	1	2	3	4	5

I'm grateful for . . .

1. _____

2. _____

3. _____

What am I most excited about today?

_____

_____

Who can I bless/encourage today?

_____

_____

Today I get to . . .

Morning

_____

Afternoon

_____

Evening

_____

Prayer requests

_____

_____

_____

One of the biggest lessons I learned when I went through a hard time was . . .

_____

_____

_____

_____

NIGHT

I felt closer to God today. ☐ Yes ☐ No

I had a positive thought life today. ☐ Yes ☐ No

I ate healthy and/or worked out today. ☐ Yes ☐ No

Where did I see God moving in my life today?

_____

_____

_____

How can I be better tomorrow?

_____

_____

_____

WEEKLY REFLECTION

In what ways did I see God move this week?

_____

_____

What is God teaching me right now?

_____

_____

Did I spend my time wisely this week?

_____

_____

Did I enjoy my life this week?

_____

_____

How can I be a blessing to someone next week?

_____

_____

How can I improve my relationship with God next week?

_____

_____

PRAISE REPORTS

_____

_____

Spread heaven
on earth.

MORNING

How do I feel?

Spiritually	1	2	3	4	5
Mentally	1	2	3	4	5
Physically	1	2	3	4	5

I'm grateful for . . .

1. _____

2. _____

3. _____

What am I most excited about today?

_____

_____

Who can I bless/encourage today?

_____

_____

Today I get to . . .

Morning

_____

Afternoon

_____

Evening

_____

Prayer requests

_____

_____

_____

When was the last time I was surprised?

_____

_____

_____

_____

NIGHT

I felt closer to God today.   ☐ Yes   ☐ No

I had a positive thought life today.   ☐ Yes   ☐ No

I ate healthy and/or worked out today.   ☐ Yes   ☐ No

Where did I see God moving in my life today?

_____

_____

_____

How can I be better tomorrow?

_____

_____

_____

MORNING

How do I feel?

Spiritually	1	2	3	4	5
Mentally	1	2	3	4	5
Physically	1	2	3	4	5

I'm grateful for . . .

1. _____

2. _____

3. _____

What am I most excited about today?

_____

_____

Who can I bless/encourage today?

_____

_____

Today I get to . . .

Morning

_____

Afternoon

_____

Evening

_____

Prayer requests

_____

_____

_____

I remember the moment I knew God was real:

_____

_____

_____

_____

NIGHT

I felt closer to God today.   ☐ Yes   ☐ No

I had a positive thought life today.   ☐ Yes   ☐ No

I ate healthy and/or worked out today.   ☐ Yes   ☐ No

Where did I see God moving in my life today?

_____

_____

_____

How can I be better tomorrow?

_____

_____

_____

MORNING

How do I feel?

Spiritually	1	2	3	4	5
Mentally	1	2	3	4	5
Physically	1	2	3	4	5

I'm grateful for . . .

1. _____

2. _____

3. _____

What am I most excited about today?

_____

_____

Who can I bless/encourage today?

_____

_____

Today I get to . . .

Morning

_____

Afternoon

_____

Evening

_____

Prayer requests

_____
_____
_____

This is what love looks like to me:

_____
_____
_____
_____

NIGHT

I felt closer to God today.   ☐ Yes   ☐ No

I had a positive thought life today.   ☐ Yes   ☐ No

I ate healthy and/or worked out today.   ☐ Yes   ☐ No

Where did I see God moving in my life today?

_____
_____
_____

How can I be better tomorrow?

_____
_____
_____

MORNING

How do I feel?

Spiritually	1	2	3	4	5
Mentally	1	2	3	4	5
Physically	1	2	3	4	5

I'm grateful for . . .

1. _____

2. _____

3. _____

What am I most excited about today?

_____

_____

Who can I bless/encourage today?

_____

_____

Today I get to . . .

Morning

_____

Afternoon

_____

Evening

_____

Prayer requests

_____

_____

_____

_____

These are the values I live by:

_____

_____

_____

_____

_____

NIGHT

I felt closer to God today.	☐ Yes ☐ No
I had a positive thought life today.	☐ Yes ☐ No
I ate healthy and/or worked out today.	☐ Yes ☐ No

Where did I see God moving in my life today?

_____

_____

_____

How can I be better tomorrow?

_____

_____

_____

MORNING

How do I feel?

Spiritually	1	2	3	4	5
Mentally	1	2	3	4	5
Physically	1	2	3	4	5

I'm grateful for . . .

1. _____

2. _____

3. _____

What am I most excited about today?

_____

_____

Who can I bless/encourage today?

_____

_____

Today I get to . . .

Morning

_____

Afternoon

_____

Evening

_____

Prayer requests

_____

_____

_____

If money were not an issue, here's how I would spend my time . . .

_____

_____

_____

_____

NIGHT

I felt closer to God today.   ☐ Yes   ☐ No

I had a positive thought life today.   ☐ Yes   ☐ No

I ate healthy and/or worked out today.   ☐ Yes   ☐ No

Where did I see God moving in my life today?

_____

_____

How can I be better tomorrow?

_____

_____

_____

MORNING

DATE: _____

How do I feel?

Spiritually	1	2	3	4	5
Mentally	1	2	3	4	5
Physically	1	2	3	4	5

I'm grateful for . . .

1. _____

2. _____

3. _____

What am I most excited about today?

_____

_____

Who can I bless/encourage today?

_____

_____

Today I get to . . .

Morning

_____

Afternoon

_____

Evening

_____

Prayer requests

_____
_____
_____

The nicest thing someone has done for me was . . .

_____
_____
_____
_____

NIGHT

I felt closer to God today.   ☐ Yes   ☐ No

I had a positive thought life today.   ☐ Yes   ☐ No

I ate healthy and/or worked out today.   ☐ Yes   ☐ No

Where did I see God moving in my life today?

_____
_____
_____

How can I be better tomorrow?

_____
_____
_____

MORNING

How do I feel?

Spiritually	1	2	3	4	5
Mentally	1	2	3	4	5
Physically	1	2	3	4	5

I'm grateful for . . .

1. _____

2. _____

3. _____

What am I most excited about today?

_____

_____

Who can I bless/encourage today?

_____

_____

Today I get to . . .

Morning

_____

Afternoon

_____

Evening

_____

Prayer requests

_____

_____

_____

One of the biggest things I appreciate about myself is . . .

_____

_____

_____

_____

NIGHT

I felt closer to God today.   ☐ Yes   ☐ No

I had a positive thought life today.   ☐ Yes   ☐ No

I ate healthy and/or worked out today.   ☐ Yes   ☐ No

Where did I see God moving in my life today?

_____

_____

_____

How can I be better tomorrow?

_____

_____

_____

WEEKLY REFLECTION

In what ways did I see God move this week?

What is God teaching me right now?

Did I spend my time wisely this week?

Did I enjoy my life this week?

How can I be a blessing to someone next week?

How can I improve my relationship with God next week?

PRAISE REPORTS

You and I
are called
to change
the world.

MORNING

How do I feel?

Spiritually	1	2	3	4	5
Mentally	1	2	3	4	5
Physically	1	2	3	4	5

I'm grateful for . . .

1. _____

2. _____

3. _____

What am I most excited about today?

_____

_____

Who can I bless/encourage today?

_____

_____

Today I get to . . .

Morning

_____

Afternoon

_____

Evening

_____

Prayer requests

_____

_____

_____

Let me think . . . Have I ever witnessed a miracle?

_____

_____

_____

_____

NIGHT

I felt closer to God today.   ☐ Yes   ☐ No

I had a positive thought life today.   ☐ Yes   ☐ No

I ate healthy and/or worked out today.   ☐ Yes   ☐ No

Where did I see God moving in my life today?

_____

_____

_____

How can I be better tomorrow?

_____

_____

_____

MORNING

How do I feel?

Spiritually	1	2	3	4	5
Mentally	1	2	3	4	5
Physically	1	2	3	4	5

I'm grateful for . . .

1. _____

2. _____

3. _____

What am I most excited about today?

_____

_____

Who can I bless/encourage today?

_____

_____

Today I get to . . .

Morning

_____

Afternoon

_____

Evening

_____

Prayer requests

_____

_____

_____

This is the one question I wish I could ask God:

_____

_____

_____

_____

NIGHT

I felt closer to God today.	☐ Yes	☐ No
I had a positive thought life today.	☐ Yes	☐ No
I ate healthy and/or worked out today.	☐ Yes	☐ No

Where did I see God moving in my life today?

_____

_____

_____

How can I be better tomorrow?

_____

_____

_____

MORNING

How do I feel?

Spiritually	1	2	3	4	5
Mentally	1	2	3	4	5
Physically	1	2	3	4	5

I'm grateful for . . .

1. _____

2. _____

3. _____

What am I most excited about today?

_____

_____

Who can I bless/encourage today?

_____

_____

Today I get to . . .

Morning

_____

Afternoon

_____

Evening

_____

Prayer requests

_____

_____

_____

I feel most courageous when . . .

_____

_____

_____

_____

NIGHT

I felt closer to God today.   ☐ Yes   ☐ No

I had a positive thought life today.   ☐ Yes   ☐ No

I ate healthy and/or worked out today.   ☐ Yes   ☐ No

Where did I see God moving in my life today?

_____

_____

_____

How can I be better tomorrow?

_____

_____

_____

MORNING

How do I feel?

Spiritually	1	2	3	4	5
Mentally	1	2	3	4	5
Physically	1	2	3	4	5

I'm grateful for . . .

1. _____

2. _____

3. _____

What am I most excited about today?

_____

_____

Who can I bless/encourage today?

_____

_____

Today I get to . . .

Morning

_____

Afternoon

_____

Evening

_____

Prayer requests

_____

_____

_____

This is one item I've purchased that makes my life easier . . .

_____

_____

_____

_____

NIGHT

I felt closer to God today.   ☐ Yes   ☐ No

I had a positive thought life today.   ☐ Yes   ☐ No

I ate healthy and/or worked out today.   ☐ Yes   ☐ No

Where did I see God moving in my life today?

_____

_____

_____

How can I be better tomorrow?

_____

_____

_____

MORNING

How do I feel?

Spiritually	1	2	3	4	5
Mentally	1	2	3	4	5
Physically	1	2	3	4	5

I'm grateful for . . .

1. _____

2. _____

3. _____

What am I most excited about today?

_____

_____

Who can I bless/encourage today?

_____

_____

Today I get to . . .

Morning

_____

Afternoon

_____

Evening

_____

Prayer requests

_____

_____

_____

The best thing that happened yesterday was . . .

_____

_____

_____

_____

NIGHT

I felt closer to God today.   ☐ Yes   ☐ No

I had a positive thought life today.   ☐ Yes   ☐ No

I ate healthy and/or worked out today.   ☐ Yes   ☐ No

Where did I see God moving in my life today?

_____

_____

_____

How can I be better tomorrow?

_____

_____

_____

MORNING

How do I feel?

Spiritually	1	2	3	4	5
Mentally	1	2	3	4	5
Physically	1	2	3	4	5

I'm grateful for . . .

1. _____

2. _____

3. _____

What am I most excited about today?

_____

_____

Who can I bless/encourage today?

_____

_____

Today I get to . . .

Morning

_____

Afternoon

_____

Evening

_____

Prayer requests

_____

_____

_____

I wish I had this skill:

_____

_____

_____

_____

NIGHT

I felt closer to God today.　　　　　　☐ Yes　☐ No

I had a positive thought life today.　　☐ Yes　☐ No

I ate healthy and/or worked out today.　☐ Yes　☐ No

Where did I see God moving in my life today?

_____

_____

_____

How can I be better tomorrow?

_____

_____

_____

MORNING

How do I feel?

Spiritually	1	2	3	4	5
Mentally	1	2	3	4	5
Physically	1	2	3	4	5

I'm grateful for . . .

1. _____

2. _____

3. _____

What am I most excited about today?

_____

_____

Who can I bless/encourage today?

_____

_____

Today I get to . . .

Morning

_____

Afternoon

_____

Evening

_____

Prayer requests

_____

_____

_____

How can I help others in my community?

_____

_____

_____

_____

NIGHT

I felt closer to God today.   ☐ Yes   ☐ No

I had a positive thought life today.   ☐ Yes   ☐ No

I ate healthy and/or worked out today.   ☐ Yes   ☐ No

Where did I see God moving in my life today?

_____

_____

_____

How can I be better tomorrow?

_____

_____

_____

WEEKLY REFLECTION

In what ways did I see God move this week?

What is God teaching me right now?

Did I spend my time wisely this week?

Did I enjoy my life this week?

How can I be a blessing to someone next week?

How can I improve my relationship with God next week?

PRAISE REPORTS

*It's good
to be here.

It's good
to be human.*

MORNING

How do I feel?

Spiritually	1	2	3	4	5
Mentally	1	2	3	4	5
Physically	1	2	3	4	5

I'm grateful for . . .

1. _____

2. _____

3. _____

What am I most excited about today?

_____

_____

Who can I bless/encourage today?

_____

_____

Today I get to . . .

Morning

_____

Afternoon

_____

Evening

_____

Prayer requests

_____

_____

_____

The part of the day I'm most grateful for is . . .

_____

_____

_____

_____

NIGHT

I felt closer to God today.   ☐ Yes   ☐ No

I had a positive thought life today.   ☐ Yes   ☐ No

I ate healthy and/or worked out today.   ☐ Yes   ☐ No

Where did I see God moving in my life today?

_____

_____

_____

How can I be better tomorrow?

_____

_____

_____

MORNING

How do I feel?

Spiritually	1	2	3	4	5
Mentally	1	2	3	4	5
Physically	1	2	3	4	5

I'm grateful for . . .

1. _____

2. _____

3. _____

What am I most excited about today?

_____

_____

Who can I bless/encourage today?

_____

_____

Today I get to . . .

Morning

_____

Afternoon

_____

Evening

_____

Prayer requests

_____

_____

_____

This is something that made me laugh today:

_____

_____

_____

_____

NIGHT

I felt closer to God today. ☐ Yes ☐ No

I had a positive thought life today. ☐ Yes ☐ No

I ate healthy and/or worked out today. ☐ Yes ☐ No

Where did I see God moving in my life today?

_____

_____

_____

How can I be better tomorrow?

_____

_____

_____

MORNING

How do I feel?

Spiritually	1	2	3	4	5
Mentally	1	2	3	4	5
Physically	1	2	3	4	5

I'm grateful for . . .

1. _____

2. _____

3. _____

What am I most excited about today?

_____

_____

Who can I bless/encourage today?

_____

_____

Today I get to . . .

Morning

_____

Afternoon

_____

Evening

_____

Prayer requests

_____

_____

_____

What does it mean to love God?

_____

_____

_____

_____

NIGHT

I felt closer to God today.   ☐ Yes   ☐ No

I had a positive thought life today.   ☐ Yes   ☐ No

I ate healthy and/or worked out today.   ☐ Yes   ☐ No

Where did I see God moving in my life today?

_____

_____

_____

How can I be better tomorrow?

_____

_____

_____

MORNING

How do I feel?

Spiritually	1	2	3	4	5
Mentally	1	2	3	4	5
Physically	1	2	3	4	5

I'm grateful for . . .

1. _____

2. _____

3. _____

What am I most excited about today?

_____

_____

Who can I bless/encourage today?

_____

_____

Today I get to . . .

Morning

_____

Afternoon

_____

Evening

_____

Prayer requests

_____

_____

_____

So far, the best part of my day today has been . . .

_____

_____

_____

_____

NIGHT

I felt closer to God today.   ☐ Yes   ☐ No

I had a positive thought life today.   ☐ Yes   ☐ No

I ate healthy and/or worked out today.   ☐ Yes   ☐ No

Where did I see God moving in my life today?

_____

_____

_____

How can I be better tomorrow?

_____

_____

_____

MORNING

How do I feel?

Spiritually	1	2	3	4	5
Mentally	1	2	3	4	5
Physically	1	2	3	4	5

I'm grateful for . . .

1. _____

2. _____

3. _____

What am I most excited about today?

_____

_____

Who can I bless/encourage today?

_____

_____

Today I get to . . .

Morning

_____

Afternoon

_____

Evening

_____

Prayer requests

_____

_____

_____

This is my salvation story.

_____

_____

_____

_____

NIGHT

I felt closer to God today.   ☐ Yes   ☐ No

I had a positive thought life today.   ☐ Yes   ☐ No

I ate healthy and/or worked out today.   ☐ Yes   ☐ No

Where did I see God moving in my life today?

_____

_____

_____

How can I be better tomorrow?

_____

_____

_____

MORNING

DATE: _____

How do I feel?

Spiritually	1	2	3	4	5
Mentally	1	2	3	4	5
Physically	1	2	3	4	5

I'm grateful for . . .

1. _____

2. _____

3. _____

What am I most excited about today?

_____

_____

Who can I bless/encourage today?

_____

_____

Today I get to . . .

Morning

_____

Afternoon

_____

Evening

_____

Prayer requests

_____

_____

_____

This is the talent that I'm most grateful for:

_____

_____

_____

_____

NIGHT

I felt closer to God today.   ☐ Yes   ☐ No

I had a positive thought life today.   ☐ Yes   ☐ No

I ate healthy and/or worked out today.   ☐ Yes   ☐ No

Where did I see God moving in my life today?

_____

_____

How can I be better tomorrow?

_____

_____

MORNING

How do I feel?

Spiritually	1	2	3	4	5
Mentally	1	2	3	4	5
Physically	1	2	3	4	5

I'm grateful for . . .

1. _____

2. _____

3. _____

What am I most excited about today?

_____

_____

Who can I bless/encourage today?

_____

_____

Today I get to . . .

Morning

_____

Afternoon

_____

Evening

_____

Prayer requests

_____

_____

_____

These are the qualities I look for in friends:

_____

_____

_____

_____

NIGHT

I felt closer to God today.   ☐ Yes ☐ No

I had a positive thought life today.   ☐ Yes ☐ No

I ate healthy and/or worked out today. ☐ Yes ☐ No

Where did I see God moving in my life today?

_____

_____

_____

How can I be better tomorrow?

_____

_____

_____

WEEKLY REFLECTION

In what ways did I see God move this week?

_____

_____

What is God teaching me right now?

_____

_____

Did I spend my time wisely this week?

_____

_____

Did I enjoy my life this week?

_____

_____

How can I be a blessing to someone next week?

_____

_____

How can I improve my relationship with God next week?

_____

_____

PRAISE REPORTS

_____

_____

Abundance,
joy,
peace,
love.

MORNING

How do I feel?

Spiritually	1	2	3	4	5
Mentally	1	2	3	4	5
Physically	1	2	3	4	5

I'm grateful for . . .

1. _____

2. _____

3. _____

What am I most excited about today?

_____

_____

Who can I bless/encourage today?

_____

_____

Today I get to . . .

Morning

_____

Afternoon

_____

Evening

_____

Prayer requests

_____

_____

_____

This is my favorite book or TV show, and why I love it . . .

_____

_____

_____

_____

NIGHT

I felt closer to God today.   ☐ Yes   ☐ No

I had a positive thought life today.   ☐ Yes   ☐ No

I ate healthy and/or worked out today.   ☐ Yes   ☐ No

Where did I see God moving in my life today?

_____

_____

How can I be better tomorrow?

_____

_____

_____

MORNING

How do I feel?

Spiritually	1	2	3	4	5
Mentally	1	2	3	4	5
Physically	1	2	3	4	5

I'm grateful for . . .

1. _____

2. _____

3. _____

What am I most excited about today?

_____

_____

Who can I bless/encourage today?

_____

_____

Today I get to . . .

Morning

_____

Afternoon

_____

Evening

_____

Prayer requests

_____

_____

_____

This one teacher has really impacted my life:

_____

_____

_____

_____

NIGHT

I felt closer to God today.   ☐ Yes   ☐ No

I had a positive thought life today.   ☐ Yes   ☐ No

I ate healthy and/or worked out today.   ☐ Yes   ☐ No

Where did I see God moving in my life today?

_____

_____

_____

How can I be better tomorrow?

_____

_____

_____

MORNING

How do I feel?

Spiritually	1	2	3	4	5
Mentally	1	2	3	4	5
Physically	1	2	3	4	5

I'm grateful for . . .

1. _____

2. _____

3. _____

What am I most excited about today?

_____

_____

Who can I bless/encourage today?

_____

_____

Today I get to . . .

Morning

_____

Afternoon

_____

Evening

_____

Prayer requests

_____

_____

_____

One memory I will always cherish is . . .

_____

_____

_____

_____

NIGHT

I felt closer to God today.   ☐ Yes   ☐ No

I had a positive thought life today.   ☐ Yes   ☐ No

I ate healthy and/or worked out today.   ☐ Yes   ☐ No

Where did I see God moving in my life today?

_____

_____

_____

How can I be better tomorrow?

_____

_____

_____

MORNING

How do I feel?

Spiritually	1	2	3	4	5
Mentally	1	2	3	4	5
Physically	1	2	3	4	5

I'm grateful for . . .

1. _____

2. _____

3. _____

What am I most excited about today?

_____

_____

Who can I bless/encourage today?

_____

_____

Today I get to . . .

Morning

_____

Afternoon

_____

Evening

_____

Prayer requests

_____

_____

_____

What do I want my legacy to be?

_____

_____

_____

_____

NIGHT

I felt closer to God today.   ☐ Yes   ☐ No

I had a positive thought life today.   ☐ Yes   ☐ No

I ate healthy and/or worked out today.   ☐ Yes   ☐ No

Where did I see God moving in my life today?

_____

_____

_____

How can I be better tomorrow?

_____

_____

_____

MORNING

DATE: _____

How do I feel?

Spiritually	1	2	3	4	5
Mentally	1	2	3	4	5
Physically	1	2	3	4	5

I'm grateful for . . .

1. _____

2. _____

3. _____

What am I most excited about today?

_____

_____

Who can I bless/encourage today?

_____

_____

Today I get to . . .

Morning

_____

Afternoon

_____

Evening

_____

Prayer requests

_____

_____

_____

The most impactful book I have ever read was . . .

_____

_____

_____

_____

NIGHT

I felt closer to God today.   ☐ Yes   ☐ No

I had a positive thought life today.   ☐ Yes   ☐ No

I ate healthy and/or worked out today.   ☐ Yes   ☐ No

Where did I see God moving in my life today?

_____

_____

_____

How can I be better tomorrow?

_____

_____

_____

MORNING

How do I feel?

Spiritually	1	2	3	4	5
Mentally	1	2	3	4	5
Physically	1	2	3	4	5

I'm grateful for . . .

1. _____

2. _____

3. _____

What am I most excited about today?

_____

_____

Who can I bless/encourage today?

_____

_____

Today I get to . . .

Morning

_____

Afternoon

_____

Evening

_____

Prayer requests

_____

_____

_____

This would be my perfect day:

_____

_____

_____

_____

NIGHT

I felt closer to God today.   ☐ Yes   ☐ No

I had a positive thought life today.   ☐ Yes   ☐ No

I ate healthy and/or worked out today.   ☐ Yes   ☐ No

Where did I see God moving in my life today?

_____

_____

_____

How can I be better tomorrow?

_____

_____

_____

MORNING

How do I feel?

Spiritually	1	2	3	4	5
Mentally	1	2	3	4	5
Physically	1	2	3	4	5

I'm grateful for . . .

1. _____

2. _____

3. _____

What am I most excited about today?

_____

_____

Who can I bless/encourage today?

_____

_____

Today I get to . . .

Morning

_____

Afternoon

_____

Evening

_____

Prayer requests

_____

_____

_____

Here's one thing that always makes me feel better:

_____

_____

_____

_____

NIGHT

I felt closer to God today.   ☐ Yes   ☐ No

I had a positive thought life today.   ☐ Yes   ☐ No

I ate healthy and/or worked out today.   ☐ Yes   ☐ No

Where did I see God moving in my life today?

_____

_____

_____

How can I be better tomorrow?

_____

_____

_____

WEEKLY REFLECTION

In what ways did I see God move this week?

_____

_____

What is God teaching me right now?

_____

_____

Did I spend my time wisely this week?

_____

_____

Did I enjoy my life this week?

_____

_____

How can I be a blessing to someone next week?

_____

_____

How can I improve my relationship with God next week?

_____

_____

PRAISE REPORTS

_____

_____

Our joy
is
heaven sent.

MORNING

How do I feel?

Spiritually	1	2	3	4	5
Mentally	1	2	3	4	5
Physically	1	2	3	4	5

I'm grateful for . . .

1. _____

2. _____

3. _____

What am I most excited about today?

_____

_____

Who can I bless/encourage today?

_____

_____

Today I get to . . .

Morning

_____

Afternoon

_____

Evening

_____

Prayer requests

_____

_____

_____

Here's everything I can see right this minute that I'm grateful for:

_____

_____

_____

_____

NIGHT

I felt closer to God today.   ☐ Yes   ☐ No

I had a positive thought life today.   ☐ Yes   ☐ No

I ate healthy and/or worked out today.   ☐ Yes   ☐ No

Where did I see God moving in my life today?

_____

_____

_____

How can I be better tomorrow?

_____

_____

_____

MORNING

How do I feel?

Spiritually	1	2	3	4	5
Mentally	1	2	3	4	5
Physically	1	2	3	4	5

I'm grateful for . . .

1. _____

2. _____

3. _____

What am I most excited about today?

_____

_____

Who can I bless/encourage today?

_____

_____

Today I get to . . .

Morning

_____

Afternoon

_____

Evening

_____

Prayer requests

_____

_____

_____

What kind of friend am I?

_____

_____

_____

_____

NIGHT

I felt closer to God today. ☐ Yes ☐ No

I had a positive thought life today. ☐ Yes ☐ No

I ate healthy and/or worked out today. ☐ Yes ☐ No

Where did I see God moving in my life today?

_____

_____

_____

How can I be better tomorrow?

_____

_____

_____

MORNING

How do I feel?

Spiritually	1	2	3	4	5
Mentally	1	2	3	4	5
Physically	1	2	3	4	5

I'm grateful for . . .

1. _____

2. _____

3. _____

What am I most excited about today?

_____

_____

Who can I bless/encourage today?

_____

_____

Today I get to . . .

Morning

_____

Afternoon

_____

Evening

_____

Prayer requests

_____

_____

_____

In the next three months, the thing I'm looking forward to the most is . . .

_____

_____

_____

_____

NIGHT

I felt closer to God today.   ☐ Yes   ☐ No

I had a positive thought life today.   ☐ Yes   ☐ No

I ate healthy and/or worked out today.   ☐ Yes   ☐ No

Where did I see God moving in my life today?

_____

_____

_____

How can I be better tomorrow?

_____

_____

_____

MORNING

How do I feel?

Spiritually	1	2	3	4	5
Mentally	1	2	3	4	5
Physically	1	2	3	4	5

I'm grateful for . . .

1. _____

2. _____

3. _____

What am I most excited about today?

_____

_____

Who can I bless/encourage today?

_____

_____

Today I get to . . .

Morning

_____

Afternoon

_____

Evening

_____

Prayer requests

_____

_____

_____

I remember the sermon that had the biggest impact on me . . .

_____

_____

_____

_____

NIGHT

I felt closer to God today. ☐ Yes ☐ No

I had a positive thought life today. ☐ Yes ☐ No

I ate healthy and/or worked out today. ☐ Yes ☐ No

Where did I see God moving in my life today?

_____

_____

_____

How can I be better tomorrow?

_____

_____

_____

MORNING

How do I feel?

Spiritually	1	2	3	4	5
Mentally	1	2	3	4	5
Physically	1	2	3	4	5

I'm grateful for . . .

1. _____

2. _____

3. _____

What am I most excited about today?

_____

_____

Who can I bless/encourage today?

_____

_____

Today I get to . . .

Morning

_____

Afternoon

_____

Evening

_____

Prayer requests

_____

_____

_____

The song that has had the biggest impact on me is . . .

_____

_____

_____

_____

NIGHT

I felt closer to God today.   ☐ Yes   ☐ No

I had a positive thought life today.   ☐ Yes   ☐ No

I ate healthy and/or worked out today.   ☐ Yes   ☐ No

Where did I see God moving in my life today?

_____

_____

_____

How can I be better tomorrow?

_____

_____

_____

MORNING

How do I feel?

Spiritually	1	2	3	4	5
Mentally	1	2	3	4	5
Physically	1	2	3	4	5

I'm grateful for . . .

1. _____

2. _____

3. _____

What am I most excited about today?

_____

_____

Who can I bless/encourage today?

_____

_____

Today I get to . . .

Morning

_____

Afternoon

_____

Evening

_____

Prayer requests

_____

_____

_____

This is the best part about my job:

_____

_____

_____

_____

NIGHT

I felt closer to God today.   ☐ Yes   ☐ No

I had a positive thought life today.   ☐ Yes   ☐ No

I ate healthy and/or worked out today.   ☐ Yes   ☐ No

Where did I see God moving in my life today?

_____

_____

_____

How can I be better tomorrow?

_____

_____

_____

MORNING

DATE: _____

How do I feel?

Spiritually	1	2	3	4	5
Mentally	1	2	3	4	5
Physically	1	2	3	4	5

I'm grateful for . . .

1. _____

2. _____

3. _____

What am I most excited about today?

_____

_____

Who can I bless/encourage today?

_____

_____

Today I get to . . .

Morning

_____

Afternoon

_____

Evening

_____

Prayer requests

As a child, I wanted to be one thing when I grew up, but as an adult, I chose something different. What changed?

NIGHT

I felt closer to God today.   ☐ Yes   ☐ No

I had a positive thought life today.   ☐ Yes   ☐ No

I ate healthy and/or worked out today.   ☐ Yes   ☐ No

Where did I see God moving in my life today?

How can I be better tomorrow?

WEEKLY REFLECTION

In what ways did I see God move this week?

_____

_____

What is God teaching me right now?

_____

_____

Did I spend my time wisely this week?

_____

_____

Did I enjoy my life this week?

_____

_____

How can I be a blessing to someone next week?

_____

_____

How can I improve my relationship with God next week?

_____

_____

PRAISE REPORTS

_____

_____

Slow down,

open your eyes,

count it all joy.

MORNING

How do I feel?

Spiritually	1	2	3	4	5
Mentally	1	2	3	4	5
Physically	1	2	3	4	5

I'm grateful for . . .

1. _____

2. _____

3. _____

What am I most excited about today?

_____

_____

Who can I bless/encourage today?

_____

_____

Today I get to . . .

Morning

_____

Afternoon

_____

Evening

_____

Prayer requests

_____

_____

_____

What is the best piece of advice I have ever received?

_____

_____

_____

_____

NIGHT

I felt closer to God today.   ☐ Yes   ☐ No

I had a positive thought life today.   ☐ Yes   ☐ No

I ate healthy and/or worked out today.   ☐ Yes   ☐ No

Where did I see God moving in my life today?

_____

_____

_____

How can I be better tomorrow?

_____

_____

_____

MORNING

How do I feel?

Spiritually	1	2	3	4	5
Mentally	1	2	3	4	5
Physically	1	2	3	4	5

I'm grateful for . . .

1. _____

2. _____

3. _____

What am I most excited about today?

_____

_____

Who can I bless/encourage today?

_____

_____

Today I get to . . .

Morning

_____

Afternoon

_____

Evening

_____

Prayer requests

_____

_____

_____

If I were famous, what would I be famous for?

_____

_____

_____

_____

NIGHT

I felt closer to God today.　　　　　☐ Yes　☐ No

I had a positive thought life today.　☐ Yes　☐ No

I ate healthy and/or worked out today.　☐ Yes　☐ No

Where did I see God moving in my life today?

_____

_____

_____

How can I be better tomorrow?

_____

_____

_____

MORNING

How do I feel?

Spiritually	1	2	3	4	5
Mentally	1	2	3	4	5
Physically	1	2	3	4	5

I'm grateful for . . .

1. _____

2. _____

3. _____

What am I most excited about today?

_____

_____

Who can I bless/encourage today?

_____

_____

Today I get to . . .

Morning

_____

Afternoon

_____

Evening

_____

Prayer requests

_____

_____

_____

The person who has made me smile the most this week is . . .

_____

_____

_____

_____

NIGHT

I felt closer to God today.   ☐ Yes   ☐ No

I had a positive thought life today.   ☐ Yes   ☐ No

I ate healthy and/or worked out today.   ☐ Yes   ☐ No

Where did I see God moving in my life today?

_____

_____

_____

How can I be better tomorrow?

_____

_____

_____

MORNING

How do I feel?

Spiritually	1	2	3	4	5
Mentally	1	2	3	4	5
Physically	1	2	3	4	5

I'm grateful for . . .

1. _____

2. _____

3. _____

What am I most excited about today?

_____

_____

Who can I bless/encourage today?

_____

_____

Today I get to . . .

Morning

_____

Afternoon

_____

Evening

_____

Prayer requests

_____

_____

_____

What does it mean to be a good listener? Am I a good listener?

_____

_____

_____

_____

NIGHT

I felt closer to God today.   ☐ Yes   ☐ No

I had a positive thought life today.   ☐ Yes   ☐ No

I ate healthy and/or worked out today.   ☐ Yes   ☐ No

Where did I see God moving in my life today?

_____

_____

_____

How can I be better tomorrow?

_____

_____

_____

MORNING

DATE: _____

How do I feel?

Spiritually	1	2	3	4	5
Mentally	1	2	3	4	5
Physically	1	2	3	4	5

I'm grateful for . . .

1. _____

2. _____

3. _____

What am I most excited about today?

_____

_____

Who can I bless/encourage today?

_____

_____

Today I get to . . .

Morning

_____

Afternoon

_____

Evening

_____

Prayer requests

_____

_____

_____

The nicest thing someone ever said to me was . . .

_____

_____

_____

_____

NIGHT

I felt closer to God today.   ☐ Yes   ☐ No

I had a positive thought life today.   ☐ Yes   ☐ No

I ate healthy and/or worked out today.   ☐ Yes   ☐ No

Where did I see God moving in my life today?

_____

_____

_____

How can I be better tomorrow?

_____

_____

_____

MORNING

How do I feel?

Spiritually	1	2	3	4	5
Mentally	1	2	3	4	5
Physically	1	2	3	4	5

I'm grateful for . . .

1. _____

2. _____

3. _____

What am I most excited about today?

_____

_____

Who can I bless/encourage today?

_____

_____

Today I get to . . .

Morning

_____

Afternoon

_____

Evening

_____

Prayer requests

_____

_____

_____

The Bible character I relate to the most is . . .

_____

_____

_____

_____

NIGHT

I felt closer to God today.   ☐ Yes   ☐ No

I had a positive thought life today.   ☐ Yes   ☐ No

I ate healthy and/or worked out today.   ☐ Yes   ☐ No

Where did I see God moving in my life today?

_____

_____

_____

How can I be better tomorrow?

_____

_____

_____

MORNING

How do I feel?

Spiritually	1	2	3	4	5
Mentally	1	2	3	4	5
Physically	1	2	3	4	5

I'm grateful for . . .

1. _____

2. _____

3. _____

What am I most excited about today?

_____

_____

Who can I bless/encourage today?

_____

_____

Today I get to . . .

Morning

_____

Afternoon

_____

Evening

_____

Prayer requests

_____

_____

_____

What do I wish I knew when I was younger that I know now?

_____

_____

_____

_____

NIGHT

I felt closer to God today.   ☐ Yes   ☐ No

I had a positive thought life today.   ☐ Yes   ☐ No

I ate healthy and/or worked out today. ☐ Yes   ☐ No

Where did I see God moving in my life today?

_____

_____

_____

How can I be better tomorrow?

_____

_____

_____

WEEKLY REFLECTION

In what ways did I see God move this week?

_____

_____

What is God teaching me right now?

_____

_____

Did I spend my time wisely this week?

_____

_____

Did I enjoy my life this week?

_____

_____

How can I be a blessing to someone next week?

_____

_____

How can I improve my relationship with God next week?

_____

_____

PRAISE REPORTS

_____

_____

Pay attention
to the good
things in life.

MORNING

DATE: _____

How do I feel?

Spiritually	1	2	3	4	5
Mentally	1	2	3	4	5
Physically	1	2	3	4	5

I'm grateful for . . .

1. _____

2. _____

3. _____

What am I most excited about today?

_____

_____

Who can I bless/encourage today?

_____

_____

Today I get to . . .

Morning

_____

Afternoon

_____

Evening

_____

Prayer requests

_____

_____

_____

What does it mean to love your neighbor?

_____

_____

_____

_____

NIGHT

I felt closer to God today.   ☐ Yes   ☐ No

I had a positive thought life today.   ☐ Yes   ☐ No

I ate healthy and/or worked out today.   ☐ Yes   ☐ No

Where did I see God moving in my life today?

_____

_____

_____

How can I be better tomorrow?

_____

_____

_____

MORNING

How do I feel?

Spiritually	1	2	3	4	5
Mentally	1	2	3	4	5
Physically	1	2	3	4	5

I'm grateful for . . .

1. _____

2. _____

3. _____

What am I most excited about today?

_____

_____

Who can I bless/encourage today?

_____

_____

Today I get to . . .

Morning

_____

Afternoon

_____

Evening

_____

Prayer requests

_____

_____

_____

What brings me peace?

_____

_____

_____

_____

NIGHT

I felt closer to God today.   ☐ Yes   ☐ No

I had a positive thought life today.   ☐ Yes   ☐ No

I ate healthy and/or worked out today.   ☐ Yes   ☐ No

Where did I see God moving in my life today?

_____

_____

_____

How can I be better tomorrow?

_____

_____

_____

MORNING

How do I feel?

Spiritually	1	2	3	4	5
Mentally	1	2	3	4	5
Physically	1	2	3	4	5

I'm grateful for . . .

1. _____

2. _____

3. _____

What am I most excited about today?

_____

_____

Who can I bless/encourage today?

_____

_____

Today I get to . . .

Morning

_____

Afternoon

_____

Evening

_____

Prayer requests

_____

_____

_____

These three people really make me feel loved:

_____

_____

_____

_____

NIGHT

I felt closer to God today.   ☐ Yes   ☐ No

I had a positive thought life today.   ☐ Yes   ☐ No

I ate healthy and/or worked out today.   ☐ Yes   ☐ No

Where did I see God moving in my life today?

_____

_____

_____

How can I be better tomorrow?

_____

_____

_____

MORNING

How do I feel?

Spiritually	1	2	3	4	5
Mentally	1	2	3	4	5
Physically	1	2	3	4	5

I'm grateful for . . .

1. _____

2. _____

3. _____

What am I most excited about today?

_____

_____

Who can I bless/encourage today?

_____

_____

Today I get to . . .

Morning

_____

Afternoon

_____

Evening

_____

Prayer requests

_____

_____

_____

There's always a silver lining. Here's the silver lining to something I'm struggling with right now:

_____

_____

_____

_____

NIGHT

I felt closer to God today. ☐ Yes ☐ No

I had a positive thought life today. ☐ Yes ☐ No

I ate healthy and/or worked out today. ☐ Yes ☐ No

Where did I see God moving in my life today?

_____

_____

_____

How can I be better tomorrow?

_____

_____

_____

MORNING

How do I feel?

Spiritually	1	2	3	4	5
Mentally	1	2	3	4	5
Physically	1	2	3	4	5

I'm grateful for . . .

1. _____

2. _____

3. _____

What am I most excited about today?

_____

_____

Who can I bless/encourage today?

_____

_____

Today I get to . . .

Morning

_____

Afternoon

_____

Evening

_____

Prayer requests

_____

_____

_____

The best news I've heard lately is . . .

_____

_____

_____

_____

NIGHT

I felt closer to God today.   ☐ Yes   ☐ No

I had a positive thought life today.   ☐ Yes   ☐ No

I ate healthy and/or worked out today.   ☐ Yes   ☐ No

Where did I see God moving in my life today?

_____

_____

_____

How can I be better tomorrow?

_____

_____

_____

MORNING

How do I feel?

Spiritually	1	2	3	4	5
Mentally	1	2	3	4	5
Physically	1	2	3	4	5

I'm grateful for . . .

1. _____

2. _____

3. _____

What am I most excited about today?

_____

_____

Who can I bless/encourage today?

_____

_____

Today I get to . . .

Morning

_____

Afternoon

_____

Evening

_____

Prayer requests

_____

_____

_____

My God-sized dreams are:

_____

_____

_____

_____

_____

NIGHT

I felt closer to God today.   ☐ Yes   ☐ No

I had a positive thought life today.   ☐ Yes   ☐ No

I ate healthy and/or worked out today.   ☐ Yes   ☐ No

Where did I see God moving in my life today?

_____

_____

_____

How can I be better tomorrow?

_____

_____

_____

MORNING

How do I feel?

Spiritually	1	2	3	4	5
Mentally	1	2	3	4	5
Physically	1	2	3	4	5

I'm grateful for . . .

1. _____

2. _____

3. _____

What am I most excited about today?

_____

_____

Who can I bless/encourage today?

_____

_____

Today I get to . . .

Morning

_____

Afternoon

_____

Evening

_____

Prayer requests

_____

_____

_____

The one person I can always count on is . . .

_____

_____

_____

_____

NIGHT

I felt closer to God today.   ☐ Yes   ☐ No

I had a positive thought life today.   ☐ Yes   ☐ No

I ate healthy and/or worked out today.   ☐ Yes   ☐ No

Where did I see God moving in my life today?

_____

_____

_____

How can I be better tomorrow?

_____

_____

_____

WEEKLY REFLECTION

In what ways did I see God move this week?

_____

_____

What is God teaching me right now?

_____

_____

Did I spend my time wisely this week?

_____

_____

Did I enjoy my life this week?

_____

_____

How can I be a blessing to someone next week?

_____

_____

How can I improve my relationship with God next week?

_____

_____

PRAISE REPORTS

_____

_____

Buy a cup of coffee for a stranger. Smile at others. Be generous with your time.

MORNING

How do I feel?

Spiritually	1	2	3	4	5
Mentally	1	2	3	4	5
Physically	1	2	3	4	5

I'm grateful for . . .

1. _____

2. _____

3. _____

What am I most excited about today?

_____

_____

Who can I bless/encourage today?

_____

_____

Today I get to . . .

Morning

_____

Afternoon

_____

Evening

_____

Prayer requests

_____

_____

_____

The one person who inspires me to love others better is . . .

_____

_____

_____

_____

NIGHT

I felt closer to God today.   ☐ Yes   ☐ No

I had a positive thought life today.   ☐ Yes   ☐ No

I ate healthy and/or worked out today.   ☐ Yes   ☐ No

Where did I see God moving in my life today?

_____

_____

_____

How can I be better tomorrow?

_____

_____

_____

MORNING

How do I feel?

Spiritually	1	2	3	4	5
Mentally	1	2	3	4	5
Physically	1	2	3	4	5

I'm grateful for . . .

1. _____

2. _____

3. _____

What am I most excited about today?

_____

_____

Who can I bless/encourage today?

_____

_____

Today I get to . . .

Morning

_____

Afternoon

_____

Evening

_____

Prayer requests

_____

_____

_____

The one thing I'm grateful of letting go of is . . .

_____

_____

_____

_____

NIGHT

I felt closer to God today.   ☐ Yes ☐ No

I had a positive thought life today.   ☐ Yes ☐ No

I ate healthy and/or worked out today. ☐ Yes ☐ No

Where did I see God moving in my life today?

_____

_____

_____

How can I be better tomorrow?

_____

_____

_____

MORNING

How do I feel?

Spiritually	1	2	3	4	5
Mentally	1	2	3	4	5
Physically	1	2	3	4	5

I'm grateful for . . .

1. _____

2. _____

3. _____

What am I most excited about today?

_____

_____

Who can I bless/encourage today?

_____

_____

Today I get to . . .

Morning

_____

Afternoon

_____

Evening

_____

Prayer requests

_____

_____

_____

How would I define faith?

_____

_____

_____

_____

NIGHT

I felt closer to God today.   ☐ Yes   ☐ No

I had a positive thought life today.   ☐ Yes   ☐ No

I ate healthy and/or worked out today.   ☐ Yes   ☐ No

Where did I see God moving in my life today?

_____

_____

_____

How can I be better tomorrow?

_____

_____

_____

MORNING

How do I feel?

Spiritually	1	2	3	4	5
Mentally	1	2	3	4	5
Physically	1	2	3	4	5

I'm grateful for . . .

1. _____

2. _____

3. _____

What am I most excited about today?

_____

_____

Who can I bless/encourage today?

_____

_____

Today I get to . . .

Morning

_____

Afternoon

_____

Evening

_____

Prayer requests

_____
_____
_____

What makes me happy?

_____
_____
_____
_____

NIGHT

I felt closer to God today.   ☐ Yes   ☐ No

I had a positive thought life today.   ☐ Yes   ☐ No

I ate healthy and/or worked out today.   ☐ Yes   ☐ No

Where did I see God moving in my life today?

_____
_____
_____

How can I be better tomorrow?

_____
_____
_____

MORNING

How do I feel?

Spiritually	1	2	3	4	5
Mentally	1	2	3	4	5
Physically	1	2	3	4	5

I'm grateful for . . .

1. _____

2. _____

3. _____

What am I most excited about today?

_____

_____

Who can I bless/encourage today?

_____

_____

Today I get to . . .

Morning

_____

Afternoon

_____

Evening

_____

Prayer requests

_____

_____

_____

Let me tell you about my favorite place in the world:

_____

_____

_____

_____

NIGHT

I felt closer to God today.   ☐ Yes   ☐ No

I had a positive thought life today.   ☐ Yes   ☐ No

I ate healthy and/or worked out today.   ☐ Yes   ☐ No

Where did I see God moving in my life today?

_____

_____

_____

How can I be better tomorrow?

_____

_____

_____

MORNING

How do I feel?

Spiritually	1	2	3	4	5
Mentally	1	2	3	4	5
Physically	1	2	3	4	5

I'm grateful for . . .

1. _____

2. _____

3. _____

What am I most excited about today?

_____

_____

Who can I bless/encourage today?

_____

_____

Today I get to . . .

Morning

_____

Afternoon

_____

Evening

_____

Prayer requests

_____

_____

_____

My favorite meal is:

_____

_____

_____

_____

NIGHT

I felt closer to God today.   ☐ Yes   ☐ No

I had a positive thought life today.   ☐ Yes   ☐ No

I ate healthy and/or worked out today.   ☐ Yes   ☐ No

Where did I see God moving in my life today?

_____

_____

_____

How can I be better tomorrow?

_____

_____

_____

MORNING

DATE: _____

How do I feel?

Spiritually	1	2	3	4	5
Mentally	1	2	3	4	5
Physically	1	2	3	4	5

I'm grateful for . . .

1. _____

2. _____

3. _____

What am I most excited about today?

_____

_____

Who can I bless/encourage today?

_____

_____

Today I get to . . .

Morning

_____

Afternoon

_____

Evening

_____

Prayer requests

_____

_____

_____

How can I be more grateful?

_____

_____

_____

_____

NIGHT

I felt closer to God today. ☐ Yes ☐ No

I had a positive thought life today. ☐ Yes ☐ No

I ate healthy and/or worked out today. ☐ Yes ☐ No

Where did I see God moving in my life today?

_____

_____

_____

How can I be better tomorrow?

_____

_____

_____

WEEKLY REFLECTION

In what ways did I see God move this week?

_____

_____

What is God teaching me right now?

_____

_____

Did I spend my time wisely this week?

_____

_____

Did I enjoy my life this week?

_____

_____

How can I be a blessing to someone next week?

_____

_____

How can I improve my relationship with God next week?

_____

_____

PRAISE REPORTS

_____

_____

Love God with
all of you.
Love your
neighbor as
yourself.
That's it.

MORNING

How do I feel?

Spiritually	1	2	3	4	5
Mentally	1	2	3	4	5
Physically	1	2	3	4	5

I'm grateful for . . .

1. _____

2. _____

3. _____

What am I most excited about today?

_____

_____

Who can I bless/encourage today?

_____

_____

Today I get to . . .

Morning

_____

Afternoon

_____

Evening

_____

Prayer requests

_____

_____

_____

If I had one superpower, what would it be?

_____

_____

_____

_____

NIGHT

I felt closer to God today.   ☐ Yes ☐ No

I had a positive thought life today.   ☐ Yes ☐ No

I ate healthy and/or worked out today.   ☐ Yes ☐ No

Where did I see God moving in my life today?

_____

_____

_____

How can I be better tomorrow?

_____

_____

_____

MORNING

How do I feel?

Spiritually	1	2	3	4	5
Mentally	1	2	3	4	5
Physically	1	2	3	4	5

I'm grateful for . . .

1. _____

2. _____

3. _____

What am I most excited about today?

_____

_____

Who can I bless/encourage today?

_____

_____

Today I get to . . .

Morning

_____

Afternoon

_____

Evening

_____

Prayer requests

_____

_____

_____

Here is one way I can bless a friend today:

_____

_____

_____

_____

NIGHT

I felt closer to God today.   ☐ Yes   ☐ No

I had a positive thought life today.   ☐ Yes   ☐ No

I ate healthy and/or worked out today.   ☐ Yes   ☐ No

Where did I see God moving in my life today?

_____

_____

_____

How can I be better tomorrow?

_____

_____

_____

MORNING

DATE: _____

How do I feel?

Spiritually	1	2	3	4	5
Mentally	1	2	3	4	5
Physically	1	2	3	4	5

I'm grateful for . . .

1. _____

2. _____

3. _____

What am I most excited about today?

_____

_____

Who can I bless/encourage today?

_____

_____

Today I get to . . .

Morning

_____

Afternoon

_____

Evening

_____

Prayer requests

_____

_____

_____

When I have bad days, I reach out to:

_____

_____

_____

_____

NIGHT

I felt closer to God today.	☐ Yes ☐ No
I had a positive thought life today.	☐ Yes ☐ No
I ate healthy and/or worked out today.	☐ Yes ☐ No

Where did I see God moving in my life today?

_____

_____

_____

How can I be better tomorrow?

_____

_____

_____

MORNING

How do I feel?

Spiritually	1	2	3	4	5
Mentally	1	2	3	4	5
Physically	1	2	3	4	5

I'm grateful for . . .

1. _____

2. _____

3. _____

What am I most excited about today?

_____

_____

Who can I bless/encourage today?

_____

_____

Today I get to . . .

Morning

_____

Afternoon

_____

Evening

_____

Prayer requests

_____

_____

_____

The best gift I ever received was . . .

_____

_____

_____

_____

NIGHT

I felt closer to God today.   ☐ Yes   ☐ No

I had a positive thought life today.   ☐ Yes   ☐ No

I ate healthy and/or worked out today.   ☐ Yes   ☐ No

Where did I see God moving in my life today?

_____

_____

_____

How can I be better tomorrow?

_____

_____

_____

MORNING

How do I feel?

Spiritually	1	2	3	4	5
Mentally	1	2	3	4	5
Physically	1	2	3	4	5

I'm grateful for . . .

1. _____

2. _____

3. _____

What am I most excited about today?

_____

_____

Who can I bless/encourage today?

_____

_____

Today I get to . . .

Morning

_____

Afternoon

_____

Evening

_____

Prayer requests

_____

_____

_____

One area of my life I'd really like to improve is . . .

_____

_____

_____

_____

NIGHT

I felt closer to God today. ☐ Yes ☐ No

I had a positive thought life today. ☐ Yes ☐ No

I ate healthy and/or worked out today. ☐ Yes ☐ No

Where did I see God moving in my life today?

_____

_____

_____

How can I be better tomorrow?

_____

_____

_____

MORNING

DATE: _____

How do I feel?

Spiritually	1	2	3	4	5
Mentally	1	2	3	4	5
Physically	1	2	3	4	5

I'm grateful for . . .

1. _____

2. _____

3. _____

What am I most excited about today?

_____

_____

Who can I bless/encourage today?

_____

_____

Today I get to . . .

Morning

_____

Afternoon

_____

Evening

_____

Prayer requests

_____

_____

_____

What does it mean to follow Jesus?

_____

_____

_____

_____

NIGHT

I felt closer to God today.   ☐ Yes   ☐ No

I had a positive thought life today.   ☐ Yes   ☐ No

I ate healthy and/or worked out today.   ☐ Yes   ☐ No

Where did I see God moving in my life today?

_____

_____

_____

How can I be better tomorrow?

_____

_____

_____

MORNING

How do I feel?

Spiritually	1	2	3	4	5
Mentally	1	2	3	4	5
Physically	1	2	3	4	5

I'm grateful for . . .

1. _____

2. _____

3. _____

What am I most excited about today?

_____

_____

Who can I bless/encourage today?

_____

_____

Today I get to . . .

Morning

_____

Afternoon

_____

Evening

_____

Prayer requests

_____

_____

_____

The basic necessity I'm most grateful for is . . .

_____

_____

_____

_____

NIGHT

I felt closer to God today.   ☐ Yes   ☐ No

I had a positive thought life today.   ☐ Yes   ☐ No

I ate healthy and/or worked out today.   ☐ Yes   ☐ No

Where did I see God moving in my life today?

_____

_____

_____

How can I be better tomorrow?

_____

_____

_____

WEEKLY REFLECTION

In what ways did I see God move this week?

_____

_____

What is God teaching me right now?

_____

_____

Did I spend my time wisely this week?

_____

_____

Did I enjoy my life this week?

_____

_____

How can I be a blessing to someone next week?

_____

_____

How can I improve my relationship with God next week?

_____

_____

PRAISE REPORTS

_____

_____

Start a
ripple of
kindness.

MORNING

How do I feel?

Spiritually	1	2	3	4	5
Mentally	1	2	3	4	5
Physically	1	2	3	4	5

I'm grateful for . . .

1. _____

2. _____

3. _____

What am I most excited about today?

_____

_____

Who can I bless/encourage today?

_____

_____

Today I get to . . .

Morning

_____

Afternoon

_____

Evening

_____

Prayer requests

_____

_____

_____

This is my most recent answered prayer:

_____

_____

_____

_____

NIGHT

I felt closer to God today.   ☐ Yes ☐ No

I had a positive thought life today.   ☐ Yes ☐ No

I ate healthy and/or worked out today.   ☐ Yes ☐ No

Where did I see God moving in my life today?

_____

_____

_____

How can I be better tomorrow?

_____

_____

_____

MORNING

How do I feel?

Spiritually	1	2	3	4	5
Mentally	1	2	3	4	5
Physically	1	2	3	4	5

I'm grateful for . . .

1. _____

2. _____

3. _____

What am I most excited about today?

_____

_____

Who can I bless/encourage today?

_____

_____

Today I get to . . .

Morning

_____

Afternoon

_____

Evening

_____

Prayer requests

_____

_____

_____

The activity that brings me the most joy is . . .

_____

_____

_____

_____

NIGHT

I felt closer to God today.   ☐ Yes   ☐ No

I had a positive thought life today.   ☐ Yes   ☐ No

I ate healthy and/or worked out today.   ☐ Yes   ☐ No

Where did I see God moving in my life today?

_____

_____

_____

How can I be better tomorrow?

_____

_____

_____

MORNING

DATE: _____

How do I feel?

Spiritually	1	2	3	4	5
Mentally	1	2	3	4	5
Physically	1	2	3	4	5

I'm grateful for . . .

1. _____

2. _____

3. _____

What am I most excited about today?

_____

_____

Who can I bless/encourage today?

_____

_____

Today I get to . . .

Morning

_____

Afternoon

_____

Evening

_____

Prayer requests

_____

_____

_____

How can I be more generous? (time or money)

_____

_____

_____

_____

NIGHT

I felt closer to God today.   ☐ Yes ☐ No

I had a positive thought life today.   ☐ Yes ☐ No

I ate healthy and/or worked out today.   ☐ Yes ☐ No

Where did I see God moving in my life today?

_____

_____

_____

How can I be better tomorrow?

_____

_____

_____

MORNING

How do I feel?

Spiritually	1	2	3	4	5
Mentally	1	2	3	4	5
Physically	1	2	3	4	5

I'm grateful for . . .

1. _____

2. _____

3. _____

What am I most excited about today?

_____

_____

Who can I bless/encourage today?

_____

_____

Today I get to . . .

Morning

_____

Afternoon

_____

Evening

_____

Prayer requests

_____

_____

_____

What do people like about me?

_____

_____

_____

_____

NIGHT

I felt closer to God today.   ☐ Yes   ☐ No

I had a positive thought life today.   ☐ Yes   ☐ No

I ate healthy and/or worked out today. ☐ Yes   ☐ No

Where did I see God moving in my life today?

_____

_____

_____

How can I be better tomorrow?

_____

_____

_____

MORNING

DATE: _____

How do I feel?

Spiritually	1	2	3	4	5
Mentally	1	2	3	4	5
Physically	1	2	3	4	5

I'm grateful for . . .

1. _____

2. _____

3. _____

What am I most excited about today?

_____

_____

Who can I bless/encourage today?

_____

_____

Today I get to . . .

Morning

_____

Afternoon

_____

Evening

_____

Prayer requests

_____

_____

_____

When was the last time I felt at peace?

_____

_____

_____

_____

NIGHT

I felt closer to God today. ☐ Yes ☐ No

I had a positive thought life today. ☐ Yes ☐ No

I ate healthy and/or worked out today. ☐ Yes ☐ No

Where did I see God moving in my life today?

_____

_____

_____

How can I be better tomorrow?

_____

_____

_____

MORNING

DATE: _____

How do I feel?

Spiritually	1	2	3	4	5
Mentally	1	2	3	4	5
Physically	1	2	3	4	5

I'm grateful for . . .

1. _____

2. _____

3. _____

What am I most excited about today?

_____

_____

Who can I bless/encourage today?

_____

_____

Today I get to . . .

Morning

_____

Afternoon

_____

Evening

_____

Prayer requests

_____

_____

_____

This is what I love most about my current season in life:

_____

_____

_____

_____

NIGHT

I felt closer to God today.   ☐ Yes   ☐ No

I had a positive thought life today.   ☐ Yes   ☐ No

I ate healthy and/or worked out today.   ☐ Yes   ☐ No

Where did I see God moving in my life today?

_____

_____

_____

How can I be better tomorrow?

_____

_____

_____

WEEKLY REFLECTION

In what ways did I see God move this week?

_____

_____

What is God teaching me right now?

_____

_____

Did I spend my time wisely this week?

_____

_____

Did I enjoy my life this week?

_____

_____

How can I be a blessing to someone next week?

_____

_____

How can I improve my relationship with God next week?

_____

_____

PRAISE REPORTS

_____

_____

Perspective
changes
everything.

90-DAY REFLECTION

Where am I now in my walk with God?

1   2   3   4   5

_____

_____

_____

_____

_____

Do I see God moving in my life?

1   2   3   4   5

_____

_____

_____

Am I more hopeful about the future?

1   2   3   4   5

_____

_____

_____

How is my mental health?

1   2   3   4   5

_____

_____

_____

_____

How do I feel physically?

1   2   3   4   5

_____

_____

_____

_____

What goals did I achieve in the past ninety days?

_____

_____

_____

_____

Which areas of my life still need improvement?

_____

_____

_____

_____

What is the most important thing I learned about myself?

_____

_____

_____

_____

_____

NOTES

NOTES

NOTES

NOTES

NOTES

NOTES

NOTES

NOTES

NOTES

NOTES

NOTES

NOTES

NOTES

NOTES

NOTES

Author and entrepreneur **Zach Windahl** has helped thousands of people better understand the Bible and grow closer to God through his company, The Brand Sunday. He's the author of several books, including *See the Good*, *The Bible Study*, *The Best Season Planner*, and *Launch with God*. Zach lives in Minneapolis, Minnesota, with his wife, Gisela, and their dog, Nyla.

MORE FROM
ZACH WINDAHL

When it comes to the future, many of us are scared of where the world is headed. *See the Good* will show you not only *how* but *why* you should focus on finding the extraordinary in everything. We're all going to face the unexplainable, but if we join Christ in our suffering, we can reap the profound benefits of living in awareness that life is a gift.

See the Good